Meditation:
A Beginner's Guide

Original title: *Seeing the Wider Picture*

Charlotte Parnell

**BARNES
& NOBLE
BOOKS**

NEW YORK

Acknowledgements

My thanks and love go:
To my beautiful and special daughters, Lucy and Kate

To Pat Gardner (an exceptional healer and spiritual teacher, friend and my surrogate mum) for her love, wisdom, support and inner beauty

To Mike Robinson (another exceptional healer and spiritual teacher of the highest order)

To Diane Holden for her friendship and love through my dark days and nights

To Julie Harper-Collins for helping me to dance again

To Anna Wilson (another exceptional healer) for her advice and for listening to me with such patience

To all my friends, family and adversaries who have been placed before me to hasten my progress on life's journey

And especially. of course
To Steve

Originally published as *Seeing the Wider Picture*

This edition published by Barnes & Noble, Inc.
by arrangement with The C. W. Daniel Company Limited.

2002 Barnes & Noble Books

ISBN 0-7607-3217-5

Printed and bound in the United States of America

05 06 07 MC 9 8 7 6

BVG

CONTENTS

Preface

I wrote this book for those who have never meditated before and equally for those who have. Use it to teach yourself, and to teach others.
Above all, teach it in our schools.
It is a lesson for life and about life.
Meditation and seeing the wider picture really *is* this simple.
Spread the word. Free yourself. Free our children.
It is written for you all with the highest and purest love.

Charlotte Parnell

Part I

SEEING THE WIDER PICTURE

The title of this part is significant for many reasons. It was chosen for me. These words were said to me by someone special about something completely different, but they resonated such a deep chord within me that my whole being shook. They were said not once, but twice, in such a way that I could never forget them. I had never heard the phrase before. These very words kick-started my rebirth into the Light.

Not only did these words start the transformation of my whole life, but their significance became more and more clear as time went by. He was meant to say them. I was meant to hear them. They were meant to ring and ring, ever louder, in my ears. The context in which they were meant was that I had to "consider the wider picture" : the consequences of my actions, but what in fact occurred was more fundamental. I was mortified and was hit at a very low point in my life. I was taken to the very edge of my existence and could take no more. It was from this point that, slowly, it was revealed to me that the picture was wider still.

That picture becomes ever wider and wider.

Sometimes we have to be plunged into the darkness in order that we may see the wider picture. It is only in this extreme that we reach out and touch the unseen hand, waiting, ever patiently, to haul us out. The process of my own rebirth is an extraordinary story, and probably the subject of a later book, where the reader will see how the jigsaw puzzle of my own life's experience had been already cut for me and how it was helped put together by this unseen hand.

It is the purpose of this book to help you find this unseen hand, without plummeting to the depths of despair as I have done. To enable you to understand, and realise for yourself, that there really is more to life than what your physical eyes can see, and what your physical ears can hear. *This* **is the wider picture**, and out there is all the help you need. It is no good me or others telling you this without you experiencing it for yourself, however much you may be open to new ideas! I cannot offer you any scientific evidence. Man needs to experience in order to learn.

It is so easy to merely accept that this is all there is. That the physical life is everything and all there ever will be; that when we are dead — that's it. In a way, it is comfortable; it explains nothing; it is easy. We do not have to strive save for physical pleasures or material things. "Science explains everything we need to know." It has become our philosopher and guide to understanding all things.

Deep within ourselves, however, and usually at times of crisis, we question this: "Why did so and so happen?" etc., and we are brought to question the very meaning of life. For some, this crisis may be a catalyst for our search, and for others, once the crisis has passed, they soon find it easier to accept it was just a coincidence, just a quirk of fate, or they find other answers acceptable and the search stops. We have free will. For some, that search can lead to embracing different philosophies or religions, or simply a complete change of lifestyle.

For me, I looked within: and there lay the answers. They were always there, they were always within me. I recognised them. It was there, within, that the wider picture was revealed to me. It was through meditation and the waking up to my own intuition that changed my life, and changed my outlook on life and my understanding of it. It enabled me to have greater control of my life. To use a rather tired, clichéd, but admittedly perfect phrase, it brought "self-empowerment". It was an absolute revelation. Not only this, but I soon began to see with my "inner eyes" and hear with my "inner ears".

I became aware of a world I could not perceive with my physical senses. Meditation helped me to shut them down so that I could discover this world, a world as real as this one: the "spiritual" world. I found that the physical plane is not the only plane in which we exist. That part of us which is here on earth has often been described as the "lower self" and that part of us which remains in spirit, as the "higher self". Our "sixth sense", our intuition — the existence of which we often acknowledge (and sometimes ignore) — is our constant bridge between these two worlds. In the discipline of meditation we can build another bridge. We can access this "spiritual" world (of which we always remain a part) from within.

The spiritual world is a world of light. I have discovered through meditation that we are basically beings of light. We half acknowledge this concept: we sometimes see the light in people's eyes, particularly when they are in love, or sense the light around them, especially saintly special people who radiate light the more they give light to others. We even have a saying: "He has seen the light" to those who acknowledge truth. We often hear mention of the aura these days, the light and colours around people; and it is something we often perceive on a physical level – we can sense that people have an "aura about them" that we either like or dislike.

When you shut your eyes in meditation and gradually develop this discipline you will be amazed at the light within. People who are full of light are usually those full of love. Meditation is a perfect vehicle for self-healing. Within it we learn to connect with the Divine light, which is a healing energy, which is love, to heal those parts of our physical and emotional and mental selves and, indeed, to direct outwards to others.

It would be easy to reject all this as a figment of my imagination, but if it is — what an imagination! You too can join in and have a wonderful time also! However, I cannot reject it as this. I have been shown this and much more, and have been constantly surprised by, yet totally at ease with, the revelations given to me in meditation and by listening to and being aware of my intuition. Join me on this journey of discovery, of self-discovery, of healing, of self-empowerment. It is relaxing. It is exciting and it is good for you.

All the exercises have been "given" to me either

within my own meditation or by spiritual teachers here on this physical plane. My thanks go to them all. None of them have I sat down and consciously made up. They are simple and special and were always meant for me to share with you, to help you. They will help you to see the wider picture. This is not a book about the spiritual teaching that has been given to me, which makes the picture wider and wider, but how you can begin to see beyond the horizon of our physical world for yourself. It is intended to be a simple manual to help get you started, on your way. Above all, I hope you *enjoy* doing the exercises in this book. They are given to you with love.

Part II

THE BACKGROUND

At the Beginning

Before you start the meditation exercises in Part III,
read this part first and also Part I, if you have
not done so already.

The Journal

Start today. Go out and buy yourself a pad of lined paper and start writing! You are going to keep a journal; not a diary of appointments, but a proper journal of your daily thoughts and feelings and whatever happens to you that day. In it you can record after each meditation what happened or what thoughts or feelings came through. Meditations are like dreams, so quickly and easily forgotten.

Write down the day and date for each entry — it sounds so obvious, but I forgot to do this at the beginning and I gradually realised it was quite important when looking back at things I had written, not only to identify the dates, but so I could see more clearly, at a later stage, how events had emerged. If you make several entries during the course of that day just leave a gap of a line, say, to show it was a separate entry for that day.

Start by writing down the trivia of the day — what you are going to do that day, what is happening, any thoughts, any feelings you want to record, or just let go of, or even something like:

"THUR 3rd June : I feel a fool writing this but I thought I'd give it a go and see what happens...I have to go to the dentist tomorrow and I am dreading it. I hate needles..."etc.

Anything. It may not seem very mind-blowing for a while, but keep at it. And anyway you will probably come to enjoy it.

You may begin to bring out negative feelings that are festering inside: anger or dislike for someone or something, either today, or in the past. Writing them down helps get them into perspective, helps you to look at them and deal with them. They are better out than in and may be emotional blocks you need to clear so you can go forward. You may find yourself writing about someone you love, or something you wish to achieve, or what you feel about something that happened in your past, or just that you forgot to put the cat out. It does not matter, so long as you start the discipline of writing daily about your thoughts and feelings.

It does not matter if you miss a day or two, so long as you get back to it as soon as possible and try to record anything significant that happened in the days you lost. It also does not matter what time of day you do it. I used to write last thing at night when everyone else was in bed and I was unlikely to be disturbed. It was a way of unwinding, relaxing, being in tune with myself, and sorting out my problems.

Why do this? We live life so fast that there is no time for reflection, for stillness. It is at moments of quiet that we begin to hear the still, small voice. In keeping a journal you set aside time for YOU. It makes space for you to contact yourself, the real you inside. You give yourself permission to express yourself and get out your feelings, and it is the most powerful method I know of you accessing your intuition. You will be amazed at what comes out!

After a while you may begin to notice a change in tone in your writing. You may perhaps start writing quite quickly, so that your pen can hardly keep up with what starts to pour out from you. You will find answers coming from within to questions or problems in your life. If you have a question — write it down. Ask, and ask for the question to be answered, within a short time if necessary. Once, I was so desperate I asked for the answer within the next ten minutes. It came within five, and I knew it was right!

Sometimes, you will write the answer down. Sometimes, you will find yourself drawn to the answer in astonishing ways. For example, you have a book you may have bought but not yet read, and you find you want to pick it up. You open it and your eye is immediately drawn to the answer! There it is staring at you. It has happened to me over and over again. Because of this, I have had the confirmation that it works, that it cannot be coincidence. I would be a fool to doubt it. I never fully believed in coincidence. Even as a child, it seemed a glib expression for phenomenal events. I cannot now accept it as a concept. Maybe Man's understanding of life and the meaning of his existence would be richer had the word "coincidence" never been thought of.

One of the first times I really noticed this bridge was a month after those words "the wider picture" were said to me. I had just started to write my journal a fortnight before and an extraordinary series of events led me to go on a day's workshop on intuition by Dr Christine Page. That is another story, but everything in it was confirmation of what I had come to realise myself. I felt I had to buy her book *The Mirror of Existence* (which I can highly recommend) and I did not open it until later that evening when I suddenly felt I had to look at it. I opened the book for the first time at page 118 (at *no* other page) and what were the very first words my eyes saw? Those three words *"the wider picture"*!

I could not believe it. There were the words again. The ones that had sent me spinning into a vortex of misery a few weeks before. How they resonated for me. Dr Page had said during her workshop, "Know that your eye is drawn to what you need to see." Those words were also bringing me out into the light. I wanted to sing and dance and tell everyone. I knew then that I was connecting with something phenomenal, but there was more, much more to come, and now I am no longer astonished by such events where others would be.

This is just one example. So it will happen to you. You might be moved to switch on the television or radio, and at that moment there is a relevant feature on a programme you need to see or hear. Another example for me was that, on another occasion, I was desperately worried about something and had been chewing it over that day and I was becoming more anxious about it. It was preying on my mind as I was driving home from school with the children, when a car overtook me on a dangerous bend. It had to pull in quickly, close in front of me, and there emblazoned on its back were the words, "No Fear". I had to laugh. They were the words I had to see and, of course, the problem was soon solved and I need not have feared.

Accessing your intuition brings a new awareness, a new dimension to your life. You may begin to feel less lonely, more in control. You may begin to understand and appreciate the positive side of that loneliness, to see the wider picture — that within even that loneliness there is a lesson in the power and wisdom of silence. That from this state comes endurance and strength and wisdom and deep inner peace, and the realisation that you are not alone, and that we are all one in spirit.

You may begin to see more of the jigsaw puzzle of your life and start to make more sense of it. You may become more aware of how connected we all are — seeing, for example, how the phone rang when you were only just thinking about someone, and that someone was the person ringing you. It certainly made me realise that people are brought into my life for a reason — to reflect some aspect of my life that I needed to deal with, perhaps, or to bring some other lesson I need to learn, or to help me change something.

Writing a journal is a daily discipline. It helps you

to set aside time for yourself and you will need to do this in meditation. It takes practice to allow time for yourself! You will find you will enjoy this writing discipline, as you will the discipline of daily meditation. Of course, there will be days when you cannot, for various reasons, find the time to write or meditate, but you will want to get back to it.

It is not necessary to fix a time of day when you will do your journal or meditation, but if you are an organised person you might find that it helps you to remember to do it and to organise everything else around it so that nothing will interfere with it. Above all, do not get stressed out by it as one more thing to remember in an already busy life. Accept the days when you cannot do it — there may be a reason for it — but try to get back to it as soon as you can.

Having said all this about journal writing, if you do not feel you want to write at all — don't. You may not feel it right for you now, or at all. I do, however, think you would increase your awareness by doing so. As a bottom line though, do write down any thoughts or feelings, or whatever impressions you had *immediately* after each meditation. As I have already indicated, you forget so quickly. You think you will remember them, but sometimes they are like dreams: soon forgotten. The thoughts that come to you in meditation may not seem significant at first, but writing them down may help you later on. The exercise will also help you discern those thoughts that are "mind-created" and those that come from your higher self. It is a simple but important exercise. Above all, trust your feelings. You may feel something to be right instinctively, whether generally, or in your writing or meditation. Learn to trust that.

What is Meditation?

I would describe it as a state of being in harmony with ourselves and the world around us. It is a state of harmonious silence. It need not be a state which you enter only if you sit in a certain position with all the paraphernalia that surrounds the practice. You do not need all this. They are options. You can do it anywhere, even on the loo!

Neither is it a mystery. You may have already experienced being in a meditative state without even realising you have, and without formally calling it anything other than feeling at peace — for example, when you were walking out in the countryside, or being lost in a beautiful piece of music. Nor need the mind be emptied of all thought as is commonly proposed. Often thoughts will come to you in the quiet and stillness from your higher self. Meditation can also be constructive, not merely passive. It is a training method to control thought processes. It is a time in which we can build, create, by directing thought.

How Often Should I Meditate

Try to do it every day. Like the journal, do not get stressed if you cannot do it but try to set a time for yourself each day for this. It is a bit like learning to play an instrument or a sport: the more you practise the easier it becomes and the more you enjoy it. But it is not a regime, it is a pleasure.

I do not think it matters what time of day you choose, although if you do it later in the evening, perhaps the more likely you are to drop off to sleep! I fit it in whenever I can, when I know I am less likely to be hassled. With my young children around I either have to wait until they are asleep or at school or whatever. When I started, there was no point in fixing a time, and I did not want to feel under pressure to achieve yet another goal in an already stressed-out life.

Furthermore, do not worry if you can only spare five minutes rather than half an hour or an hour. It does not matter. Sometimes that mere five minutes can refresh you or give you something more profound than a longer period, and that short time can feel like much longer.

The Atmosphere for Meditation

Do not get hung up about getting the atmosphere right. I have meditated in the most unlikely settings and still enjoyed it. If you have the time and money, and you think it will help you, then perhaps consider buying some relaxing music. It is not necessary, but there did come a time when I needed to do this; I felt it was right. When the tape came to an end, it would remind me of the time and I would prepare to come out of meditation. I often like to meditate outside in the sunshine, feeling the warmth of the sun on the back of my neck. Fresh air, if warm and not distracting, is a bonus during meditation. I sometimes light a candle, perhaps a scented one, and I can use it to close the meditation. I have only used incense a few times because I found it overpowering and therefore distracting. Scented candles are usually more gentle. Obviously, great care must be taken to ensure that any candle is placed in a safe position, away from draughts or anything that might catch alight or might knock it over. It must always be placed in an appropriate candle-holder. I prefer scented candles that come in their own tin holder, which I then place, for safety, within a bowl. Be wise, be safe.

I have done meditations in groups where Tibetan bells have been used to bring a meditation to a close. They have a wonderful vibration and it feels as if the air is being cleansed around you. I have a music tape where they appear in one section and during meditation I have found that they help me to clear the junk thoughts crowding my mind and redirect my thoughts and relax more deeply.

Position

The main criterion for meditation is to be comfortable. This will enable you to forget your physical body and your surroundings. To begin with, choose the room or location in which you think you will relax the most, if you can. Someone once said to me, "I'd love to meditate but I can't sit cross-legged." This completely surprised me and brought home to me the general misconception about meditation. I think that those people patiently fishing by the side of a lake, lost in a world of their own, are doing a form of meditation without calling it so.

I do not think it makes any difference if you sit in a chair, lie down, or sit cross-legged, or manage to contort even that position into a yogic one. I have even meditated standing up on occasions. After all, t'ai chi is a meditation, a moving meditation on your feet. If you sit in a chair, try and make sure that you sit with your spine as straight as possible. Use cushions to support your back if necessary. The same goes for sitting cross-legged. If I am in this position, I sit on a soft cushion with my back supported by the side of the bed. Sitting as straight as you can comfortably manage helps to release the ribcage and lets you have more space to breathe. It makes it more effortless.

If you sit on a chair, or lie down on the bed, do not cross your legs — this disrupts the flow of energy, as well as your circulation. Do not cross your arms either, but find a comfortable position for them: rest them on the arms of your chair, or put your hands on each of your thighs. Sometimes I cup my right hand under my left hand in my lap. Sometimes that just feels right and helps me feel centred.

I often start a meditation cross-legged but feel one of my legs go numb after a while so I have to stretch it out to the side. This does not matter and does not disrupt the meditation at all. You *are* allowed to move in meditation — you do not have to sit stock-still. If you need to scratch your leg, do it!

You can also buy, or make (if you are handy with a saw), a Zen bench. These are small wooden sloping stools that enable you to kneel so that your back is straight, but your weight is taken by sitting on the sloping stool. Your lower legs slip comfortably under the seat of the stool. You will often see them advertised in the back of New-Age magazines in their classified section.

Breathing

The first thing we do when we come into the world is to take our first breath. The breath is the first step you take to withdraw from it.

Most of us are lazy about breathing; (I include myself in this!) But taking the trouble to breathe more slowly and more deeply will really help you relax. In antenatal classes, it is widely recognised that breath control can substantially assist relaxation and the birth process. It has health benefits too, in getting more oxygen around the bloodstream. It slows down your heart rate and can be used to assist you in concentrating and letting go of the myriad of thoughts crowding your mind. If my mind does wander into trivia, which it irritatingly does sometimes, with a few deep breaths I can let go again and get back into a meditative state once more.

You can use the breath to really let go of all those troubles and pressures on you, so that you can rise above them. This is sometimes described as being part of the process of "raising your consciousness" and, in a sense, you are: you are leaving the earthly problems behind (down there, so to speak) so that you can just be you, free from it all to embrace your "higher self" — the real you. Now I only have to take one or two deep breaths and I can completely let go.

So, remember, get your posture right, be comfortable and do not skip the instructions on the breath at the beginning of the exercises in Part III, until you feel you can really let go and relax in your own way. The breath is there to help you.

Relaxation

Having done all this, to begin with you may wage a battle with yourself and get into a fluster because you still cannot relax. Do not worry! Do not allow yourself to be put off. The lower mind will throw anything at you, it seems, to stop you from releasing yourself from its grasp. It can be tenacious in its grip. The best advice I can give is either go back to concentrating on the breath in the exercises

I have given you, or just ask inwardly for help to get rid of the thoughts plaguing you (and help will be given), or just go with them. You may just have to accept that today is not the day for you to "slip away", or you could just let the thoughts come and go anyway.

I confess that there have been times when my head has been so full of nonsense, worries and dreams that I have sat for half an hour or so, unable to get away from them. Sometimes, that is as far as I have got. At others, suddenly, it is as if the mind has got tired of its own effort and a wonderful stillness has come upon me. No thoughts, no feelings, just being — I have gone into a deep meditative state without really trying! So do not try too hard! Do not be intense about it — one stage will lead to the next. Furthermore, to begin with, do not meditate for too long a time if possible. Remember, it is the start of a process.

The "point of stillness" is one of the goals in meditation. It may only be for a flash of a second, or it may last a little longer, but it is truly blissful and worth the "effort". You may in this stillness experience nothing but a sort of celestial peace, but it is like a glimpse of something precious and wondrous that you must see and experience more of. You might have something more profound revealed to you or you may be simply just amazed that for the first time for ages you felt truly relaxed because your busy mind had finally shut up!

Furthermore, when the conscious mind really lets go, the body will be allowed to heal itself more effectively. When you are asleep at night, just think of the healing that takes place in the physical body while the mind is away with the fairies!

I am not saying you need to have no thoughts at all to be in a meditative state. This point of stillness does not happen all the time. Sometimes, you might make more sense of the thoughts that crowd your mind. You might realise the meaning, the significance, of what you are thinking of. The thoughts may also help you realise an aspect of your true self, or what you have to let go of or deal with in your physical life. You may experience a deeper wisdom of extraordinary profundity, perhaps about the illusion of life here on Earth: that life is topsy-turvy; that we are spirit first, physical body second; that we are in truth all one — individuated beings of light but all of the one light...but these are other stories...you see, the picture gets ever wider and wider!

Through the heart wisdom and truth comes. The meditation exercises I have given you will help you build a temple in your heart for you to retreat to, to learn in, to rebuild in, to create in and to express and feel deepest love.

Visualisation in meditation is a way of controlling and directing thought. In this creation something may be revealed to you in the same way as if you were free of thought at that point of stillness. You may still be in a deep meditative state, even though your mind is "working" because you have let go of the trivia and troubles that crowd your mind and are truly relaxed.

I must add that you can be in a deep meditation and still be aware of the sounds around you. You do not have to be "out" completely as if you were asleep.

You may still remain very much in the physical. Indeed, you may need to move a part of your body within a meditation exercise (as in Exercise Four). This often occurs in self-healing meditations.

I have not included in these exercises any chanting to help you let go and relax. This method is wonderful and I have been to a healing workshop using chanting, and was astonished at its power. It is, however, very difficult to fully get across the sound and effect in a book! I hope that this is something that may, at some time, feel right for you to explore. I have chanted using the "owm" in one long breath and using the sounds "oo-or-aye-ay-ee" in one breath again and again for about three or four minutes, on my own and in groups. It is a lovely way to relax.

Visualisation and Thought

It is in this lovely, relaxed state that you may become aware of the light inside of you. I have given you exercises to help you explore and to develop this. This is the energy of life itself. It is love. It is divine. It is healing energy. I have given you exercises to use it for self-healing. All the exercises involve visualisation: in other words, using your imagination — creating pictures within your mind's eye of what you want to happen, what you want to see.

Do not doubt the creative power of this tool. Always remember: *thought creates reality*. Do not doubt this. (After all, consider this: if we are a product of God's imagination, we are therefore a part of God himself. It follows that He cannot be separate from us and we therefore have His attributes and His creative power. Are we not therefore mini-gods?) You do not have to be in a meditative state to create with your imagination, your thoughts, a physical reality of what is in your head. We are only just on the threshold of discovering this. For example, we are now realising the value of positive thought with regard to a state of wellbeing in the same way that our negativity can make us ill. Our bodies are full of the energy of our thoughts. We have to be careful how we think!

Matthew Manning, a well-known healer, once showed me in a presentation a revelatory exercise that makes a clear and immediate demonstration of this fact. He asked a man, who he did not know, to stand in front of him, and then he asked whether he was right- or left-handed. He asked him to put out his weakest arm horizontally and to think of something positive, something that would make him happy, bring him great joy. When he had this thought in his mind, Matthew told the man that he was going to force his arm to go back down by his side and the man was to try to resist him. Try as he could, Matthew could not budge the arm. Then the man put out his strongest arm and Matthew got him to fix in his mind a negative thought, something that would make him sad and miserable. When he had done this Matthew told the man to again resist Matthew's efforts to force that arm back to the man's side. There was hardly any resistance. You too can try this out for yourselves and see the extraordinary effect of the attitude of mind.

Like attracts like. Think negative thoughts and a

negative reality you will create for yourself. You will create illness (dis-ease) eventually within your physical body, because your mind is not in a harmonious state. Think right thoughts. Think happy thoughts. Think positive and believe in it. I have learnt to start each day afresh as if it were a new life. Learn to let go of the past with joy. Live each day as if it were your last. Live life joyfully. You are special. You deserve it. You are meant to be happy. Happiness = holiness = wholeness = health.

Apply love to your issues and see what happens. Above all, let fear go. It filters the light/love. Fear is Man's greatest enemy, more than anyone else or anything else. It is important to let it go and any other negative feelings on a day to day basis. Do not be a victim of your own thought processes. Take what you need from life's experiences, chuck out what you do not.

If there are negative incidents in your life, recreate them into positive ones. Think: "If I could raise my head and peer above the parapet of the castle of my physical world, what would I see?

Would I view things differently, looking down on it and beyond the horizons? What opportunity have I been given? What is the other perspective on what is happening?" In this way, it may be easier to look, not at what you have lost in any bad experience, but what you have gained. It is hard, I know, to get one's head above the parapet sometimes and keep one's vision clear, but meditation helps that.

When you create in your imagination a picture, you are creating a reality within. When you "see" the light within or a picture of something, it is real, it is happening. You are creating energy, and more advanced spiritual teaching will explain how this thought form can come into being in the physical world. Thoughts are things. Thought = energy. They do not stay in your physical skull! These energy forms are sent out into the universe (energy-matrix, if you like), and can create form, become manifest.

I shall never forget witnessing this energy when I walked through my own anger. I was furious about something and was amazed to see sparks of light all around me. It stopped me in my tracks.

Once, one of my daughters had left something at school and was howling with fury. I saw these same sparks of light being thrown off her as I walked past her. I had walked through them. So, sparks really do fly in an argument – it is not just a saying.

As I have indicated, creating with your imagination is a powerful tool and can only be used with love. To do otherwise would harm you. "Do unto others as you would have done unto yourself" (in thought, word and deed), is a statement loaded with spiritual meaning and must be obeyed.

Words are powerful expressions of our thoughts. They carry the energy of our thoughts. They are a manifestation of them. So be very careful too with what you say. That is why positive daily affirmations are so powerful, and can really help in the healing process. An example of a positive affirmation is, "I am well, I am healthy."

I learnt the hard way about the effect of negative and positive affirmations! After the breakdown of my marriage, my self-esteem was at an all-time low. I was guilty of repeating to myself a daily silent mantra that I was useless, not good enough for anything or anyone. A patch of eczema had appeared on my back behind my heart. Effectively, I had been stabbing myself in the back.

One morning, at about 11 am, I looked at myself in the mirror and noticed that it had got much bigger. In an instant, it came to me what I was doing to myself. It was beginning to look like the psoriasis my mother had had down her spine. She had a very low self-esteem, and it just clicked. I was angry with myself, and vowed not to say these things to myself about myself ever again. I repeated over and over, "I AM good enough, I AM worthy."

I kept up this positive mantra and, with my head held high, I went into town at about lunch-time. I was drawn into a bookshop. Suddenly I wanted to look at a book by Louise L. Hay called *You Can Heal Your Life* which I had seen about a year previously. On that occasion its style did not appeal to me and I did not purchase it, but I suddenly felt that it deserved another look. I took the book off the shelf and opened it at random. I opened it (at no other page) at page 78 and the first words I saw were in block capitals: "I APPROVE OF MYSELF." It was just the confirmation I needed. Needless to say, I bought the book. By 4 pm that same afternoon, the patch on my back had almost completely gone!

Self-Healing

Love heals. It heals not only our emotions but also our physical state. It is the light that casts out the shadows of darkness, of fear, of illness, of dis-ease. To live one's life with love flowing freely is the perfect state of being. "But of course we cannot do this," I hear you say. We can, and every day we can make a new start, a fresh start at it. We have to practise the practice of letting in the Light, letting in this Divine love. It is so powerful and beautiful and with it comes wisdom and truth.

I have been privileged to channel this healing light to others since I was only fourteen years old. I have seen it so many times with my physical eyes and my "inner" eyes. I am not a fool. I can see it and feel it. It does not come from me. I am merely the jump-lead that connects up the depleted battery to the Source. The person receiving it sometimes feels it, or "sees" it, too. You can, with your powerful tool, your imagination, visualise it travelling via your heart to those parts of your physical body you wish to mend. You can even feel its warmth sometimes; it moves like liquid sunshine.

You can send this light, this love, this energy, anywhere, even around the world, with your thought, by just sending it wherever you want in your mind, and it will be so. This is called distant, or absent, healing. I have (without prior knowledge of it being sent) received absent healing from other people and I have been able to say the exact times at which they were sending it because I have been able to feel it so strongly. Some of those sending it were delighted and astonished at my confirmation of their efforts — they had only hoped their loving thoughts would have some effect without ever being given precise confirmation before. What a different world it would be if we all practised this for each other. I do not believe this is fantasy, some hippy dream. Having seen and felt the power of this love, I know it is real.

We have all seen love in action. You cannot scientifically measure it: there is no "loveometer" yet, but we know it exists. Even the most cynical person is not immune to the emotion of love and understands it has an "energy" of something. We have all seen its healing power in action: the child with a cut knee is comforted in the arms of its mother, who pours out her love to it, and within a minute that child is desperate to get down and be off playing again. We know that we feel better when surrounded by love.

It never ceases to amaze me when listening to the radio the amount of songs written about the power of love and the light within us. We recognise it without understanding its significance. I have referred to it as Divine love, because that is what I believe it is, but it is not a prerequisite that you think this, or believe in God, before you can tap into it. We all know wonderful, kind, gentle people who are full of love and generosity for others, but who are atheists. I know several healers who do not believe in God, but know and understand that the energy they channel does not come from them. They recognise, however, that it comes from a universal source of energy, of healing energy, somewhere.

Through the meditation exercises I have set out, you can practise letting in this wonderful light and start healing. One little exercise I was taught (by Mike Robinson, a wonderful spiritual teacher), which I sometimes use if I do not have time to meditate but feel stressed out, is this: take yourself outside and imagine you have plugs in the soles of your feet. Imagine you are taking out those plugs and letting all the stress, the blackness, drain out into the earth until you "see" it all gone. Put back in the plugs and then imagine you are being filled with a beautiful white light through the top of your head. You may be surprised how much better you feel! Alternatively, if you have difficulty in letting go of negative thoughts, just imagine them floating away from you in a bubble of light and then just pop the bubble. Easy.

I also use the white light, if I am in any threatening situation, to protect myself. I simply imagine myself surrounded by a bubble of white light that comes down from above my head, encircling me. If I am driving my car I sometimes imagine this and ask inwardly for protection while I make the journey. I sometimes do it even before I get out of bed in the morning.

I have described the healing light in this section and how you can visualise it, and use it. However, it is NOT an alternative to going and seeing a doctor if you need to. This may sound obvious but I must make this clear. Your doctor is there to help you and should be contacted straight away if you need to. Neither is it an alternative to any medication he may prescribe. We need all the help we can get!

The Benefits of Meditation

These are well-documented already. We know that the act of breathing deeply increases our oxygen intake which helps us relax and enables the body to work more efficiently. It slows down the heart rate and reduces stress. It has been claimed that it boosts the immune system. I know that I feel healthy most of the time. It has been claimed also that it slows down the ageing process. As I am nearly forty, this is a bonus! More importantly, it has brought to me:

Strength	:	the inner strength to deal with whatever daily tests I have to face
Insight	:	an understanding of my situation, or those of others, and a greater understanding of my life and its mysteries
Peace of mind	:	an inner peace, a calm acceptance of the tests I am facing, knowing that I have free will in how I choose to deal with them, the inner strength to do so, and all the help I need — I only have to ask
Silence	:	a rare and beautiful commodity

Appreciation	:	and wonder at the world around me and the world within
Relaxation	:	it is a time to rest and slip away from all my troubles and endless things to do. It is a time for me. Even if I only get a good nights sleep, then it has been worth it
Self-healing	:	using visualisation, I can direct the light, the healing light, to those areas of my body that need it. I can rebuild with the light
Pleasure	:	I would not bother if I did not find it so pleasurable!

If you get back any one of these benefits then it will be an added bonus: it will be worth your time.

Above all, I hope this book helps you to see beyond the restrictive frame of your physical life, and brings to you the added dimension of the wider picture. May it be the start of a wondrous journey for you.

Part III

THE MEDITATION
EXERCISES

If you have never practised meditation before, do not pick out the exercise you wish to do first, but work through the exercises methodically. I have set them out in an order so that you can gradually get to feel what it is like.

I have read other meditation exercises that get you to breathe in through the nose and out through the mouth. Personally, I would find this extremely tiresome and distracting, when the object is to forget about the physical body. In the exercises I have set out for you, just breathe in and out through your nose, as you would normally.

Read through each exercise before you start it. They are simple and should be easy to remember. Once you have done the exercise a few times you will not need the book. Have the book in front of you to begin with, however. If you lose your way, just open your eyes and look at the sentences to the left-hand side of the page.

It really IS all right to open your eyes if you need to! I have often come out of meditation, answered the telephone and gone straight back into meditation immediately afterwards.

As an alternative, put the exercise onto a tape as you would wish it to be read to you and play that. Make sure to pause between each step and give yourself enough time to see / imagine what you are instructed to see.

As you work through the exercises, you may find one that suits you best and is just right for you, at this time. If so, stick with it until you feel you want to move onto the next. As you move on, you may find an aspect of one of the exercises you have previously done that suited you and you may wish to incorporate that into a later exercise: this is fine, whatever you feel comfortable with.

The first exercise is just to get you used to seeing the light and seeing yourself immersed in it. Seeing the light coming down through the top of your head and down into the heart, is what I call my "core" meditation. It is basic. It is simple. It is easy to grasp and easy to visualise. If you cannot see the light with your inner vision — do not despair, it will come with practice — in the meantime, just imagine that it IS there. As you progress and find your own style, you may always use it to start a meditation if you wish, as it brings the light down into the heart, where it needs to be.

Learn and practise the counted breath method in Exercise Two, but you do not have to count the inhale and exhale breath if you find that difficult. You can just see the light travel down through the crown of your head, down your spine and into your heart, in your own time (as in Exercise Three). The method of counting the inhale and exhale breath is sometimes a useful discipline to use where the mind is having difficulty in settling, and is therefore good to learn. It will also help you to slow your breathing down and to use more of your lung capacity.

In each exercise, I have given you the same

method of how to close the meditation. It is simple and it will come automatically to you once you have done it a few times. This closing is very important. *Do not forget it*. When you meditate your energy centres will start to open up automatically. This closing exercise will give you the protection you need so that they will not be damaged or harmed when you come out of meditation. Learn it well and ALWAYS use it. Never finish a meditation without it. It is so simple that you have no excuse not to really. It also has the added benefit of grounding you so that you will not feel "spaced out" afterwards.

For the first few exercises, the beginning elements are similar. This is to help you experience the light and to enable you to establish a routine, so that you will not have to worry much about how to begin.

If you have trouble imagining this golden light, just think of the golden flame of a candle (which matches its intensity), or the beautiful shafts of golden sunlight you might see in woodland (which captures its beauty and peace). It has the gentle warmth of sweet sunshine and it is full of love.

These exercises can take as little as five minutes, if you want, by taking shorter pauses and without meandering off with extraneous thoughts. You can do them on the train, at lunch breaks at work or at school, as you get up, before you go to bed, whatever. You can make them last longer if you wish by lengthening the pauses between each step or by taking a long pause before closing. Here, however, is a word of warning — I have often meditated thinking I have only been doing it for fifteen minutes, only to find that I have been "out" for over an hour. In the meditative state, your concept of time has no meaning. It is a man-made creation and has no relevance within.

If you are lighting a candle during a meditation, when you come out of it and before you blow it out, think of someone you know who needs help or healing and imagine them standing bathed in the golden light of your candle flame. See them well and happy in that light. Ask inwardly that the golden healing light (like the light of your candle) be given to that person if they wish it to be, then blow it out. In this simple way, you are sending beautiful healing light to others.

So, before you start, get comfortable, get your posture right and relax.

Enjoy it!

☼ Exercise One

BREATHE — SEE THE SUN — BREATHE IT IN — CLOSE

Close your eyes

Let out a big sigh : As you do so think of yourself
letting go of any stress or
negative thought you are
holding onto.

Repeat the sigh : Let it go.

Breathe in slowly : A deep breath in.

Breathe out slowly : As you do so, let go. Let go of
all the troubles and trivia that
you are holding in your mind
at this time. Forget them. You
do not need them at this time.
This is your time. Let them go.

Repeat the slow
breathing above

Repeat again : Really let go of all these
thoughts. Feel your body
gently relaxing. Be at peace.
If you need to, say it,
"Be at peace."

Imagine you are sitting in the sunshine	:	Whether on your favourite beach, in a field, or garden, or woodland area — wherever you feel happiest.
Feel the warmth of the sun	:	Feel it on the top of your head, on your shoulders.
See that sun	:	See its golden light above you, with your imagination, with your mind.
See that golden light	:	See it just above the top of your head, again with your imagination.
Let the light embrace you	:	Feel it all around you. You are immersed in it.
Breathe in the light	:	As you slowly breathe in, imagine this golden light filling your heart, entering your heart through your chest wall.
Hold the golden light in your heart	:	See it with your imagination. Feel it. Feel its warmth. Feel its peace and the love it brings you.

To close : **Imagine a spiral of white light come up from the earth below you, encircling you seven times, in a clockwise direction. When it gets to the top of your head, see it enter the top of your head and go back to the earth below you, via your spine. Be very aware of your feet on the ground or what you are lying upon.**

This is an important part of the exercise — it will "ground" you and help you feel less spaced out.

☼ Exercise Two

BREATHE — SEE THE SUN — BREATHE IT IN WITH
COUNTED BREATH — CLOSE

Close your eyes

Let out a big sigh	:	As you do so think of yourself letting go of any stress or negative thought you are holding onto.
Repeat the sigh	:	Let it go.
Breathe in slowly	:	A deep breath in.
Breathe out slowly	:	As you do so, let go. Let go of all the troubles and trivia that you are holding in your mind at this time. Forget them. You do not need them at this time. This is your time. Let them go.
Repeat the slow breathing above		
Repeat again	:	Really let go of all these thoughts. Feel your body gently relaxing. Be at peace. If you need to, say it, "Be at peace."

Imagine you are sitting in the sunshine	:	Whether on your favourite beach, in a field, or garden, or woodland area — wherever you feel happiest.
Feel the warmth of the sun	:	Feel it on the top of your head, on your shoulders.
See that sun	:	See its golden light above you, with your imagination, with your mind.
See that golden light	:	See it just above the top of your head, again with your imagination.

Breathe in deeply
for a count of six

Breathe out for a
count of eight

Pause

Repeat this counted breath	:	But this time imagine as you breathe in you are **breathing in the sunlight** through the top of your head to your forehead for six counts. **As you breathe out**, imagine that golden light travelling down your head, throat

and chest into your **heart** for
eight counts.

Hold the light in
your heart for a
few moments

Repeat this counted : Repeat it five or six times.
breath of sunlight   Imagine the golden light filling
your heart. Feel its warmth.
Relax for a few minutes. Let
your thoughts come and go. Let
them go. Be at peace. If you feel
any stressful thoughts returning,
breathe in the sunlight again.

To close   : **Imagine a spiral of white
light come up from the earth
below you, encircling you
seven times, in a clockwise
direction. When it gets to the
top of your head, see it enter
the top of your head and go
back to the earth below you,
via your spine. Be very aware
of your feet on the ground or
what you are lying upon.**

This is an important part of
the exercise – it will "ground"
you and help you feel less
spaced out.

☼ Exercise Three

BREATHE IN THE SUN — FROM THE HEART TO THE
BODY — CLOSE

Close your eyes

Let out a big sigh	:	As you do so think of yourself letting go of any stress or negative thought you are holding onto.
Repeat the sigh	:	Let it go.
Breathe in slowly	:	A deep breath in.
Breathe out slowly	:	As you do so, let go. Let go of all the troubles and trivia that you are holding in your mind at this time. Forget them. You do not need them at this time. This is your time. Let them go.
Repeat the slow breathing above		
Repeat again	:	Really let go of all these thoughts. Feel your body gently relaxing. Be at peace. If you need to, say it, "Be at peace."

63

Imagine you are sitting in the sunshine	:	Whether on your favourite beach, in a field, or garden, or woodland area — wherever you feel happiest.
Feel the warmth of the sun	:	Feel it on the top of your head, on your shoulders.
See that sun	:	See its golden light above you, with your imagination, with your mind.
See that golden light	:	See it just above the top of your head, again with your imagination.
Breathe in that sunlight into your heart	:	You can use the counted-breath method in Exercise Two if you want to, or just see it with your imagination move down through the top of your head and down into your heart as you deeply breathe. It need only take you a few slow, relaxing breaths. That sunlight is pure energy, a pure, loving and peaceful energy.
Hold the light in your heart	:	Leave it there for a few moments, see it there, a beautiful golden light.

Let the light slowly
expand in your heart

Let the light expand : See your body filled with
and slowly spread   beautiful golden light.
to all parts of
your body

Send more light
from your heart to
those areas of your
body you feel need
healing, or a boost

To close   : **Imagine a spiral of white
                           light come up from the earth
                           below you, encircling you
                           seven times, in a clockwise
                           direction. When it gets to the
                           top of your head, see it enter
                           the top of your head and go
                           back to the earth below you,
                           via your spine. Be very aware
                           of your feet on the ground or
                           what you are lying upon.**

                           I repeat — this is an important
                           part of the exercise — it will
                           "ground" you and help you
                           feel less spaced out.

☀ Exercise Four

"THE JEWEL"

Close your eyes

Let out a big sigh	:	As you do so think of yourself letting go of any stress or negative thought you are holding onto.
Repeat the sigh	:	Let it go.
Breathe in slowly	:	A deep breath in.
Breathe out slowly	:	As you do so, let go. Let go of all the troubles and trivia that you are holding in your mind at this time. Forget them. You do not need them at this time. This is your time. Let them go.
Repeat the slow breathing above		
Repeat again	:	Really let go of all these thoughts. Feel your body gently relaxing. Be at peace. If you need to, say it, "Be at peace."

Imagine you are sitting in the sunshine	:	Whether on your favourite beach, in a field, or garden, or woodland area — wherever you feel happiest.
Feel the warmth of the sun	:	Feel it on the top of your head, on your shoulders.
See that sun	:	See its golden light above you, with your imagination, with your mind.
See that golden light	:	See it just above the top of your head, again with your imagination.
Let the light embrace you	:	Feel it all around you. You are immersed in it.
Cup your right hand and raise it so it is held in front of your heart	:	Do this physically with your right hand, when you are ready and feel at peace in the light.
Imagine there is a beautiful jewel placed in that hand	:	See its colour or colours. See it radiate fabulous light.
Imagine that jewel radiate golden light	:	Imagine it surrounded by golden light. See, in your mind, your cupped hand full of this golden light.

Gently draw your
cupped hand toward
your heart. Cup your
hand over your heart
and hold it there

Imagine that jewel : See it, with your mind, inside
now placed directly   your heart, radiating its
in your heart   beautiful golden light. It is there
                       for you always. Whenever you
                       feel you need strength, love,
                       peace or wisdom, remember
                       that jewel is in your heart:
                       always radiating this love for
                       you. It is your gift.

To close : **Imagine a spiral of white light
           come up from the earth below
           you, encircling you seven times,
           in a clockwise direction. When it
           gets to the top of your head, see
           it enter the top of your head and
           go back to the earth below you,
           via your spine. Be very aware of
           your feet on the ground or what
           you are lying upon.**

           I repeat — this is an important
           part of the exercise — it will
           "ground" you and help you
           feel less spaced out.

☼ Exercise Five

"THE CANDLE"

Close your eyes

Let out a big sigh : As you do so think of yourself letting go of any stress or negative thought you are holding onto.

Repeat the sigh : Let it go.

Breathe in slowly : A deep breath in.

Breathe out slowly : As you do so, let go. Let go of all the troubles and trivia that you are holding in your mind at this time. Forget them. You do not need them at this time. This is your time. Let them go.

Repeat the slow
breathing above

Repeat again : Really let go of all these thoughts. Feel your body gently relaxing. Be at peace. If you need to, say it, "Be at peace."

Imagine you are sitting in the sunshine	:	Whether on your favourite beach, in a field, or garden, or woodland area — wherever you feel happiest.
Feel the warmth of the sun	:	Feel it on the top of your head, on your shoulders.
See that sun	:	See its golden light above you, with your imagination, with your mind.
See that golden light	:	See it just above the top of your head, again with your imagination.
Let the light embrace you	:	Feel it all around you. You are immersed in it.
In your mind, picture in front of you a white lighted candle	:	Imagine it, in front of you, level with your heart. See its golden flame. Look at the intensity of that golden light. Feel it radiate that light towards your heart.
In your mind, draw the lighted candle into your heart	:	See it placed in your heart, radiating its golden light, dispelling all fear, giving you courage, and healing. It will always be there for you.

If you feel your mind try to blow it out, imagine golden light above your head — draw that light.in through the top of your head down into your heart	:	You may imagine a shaft of golden light from the top of your head to the heart. This light is like oxygen to the flame and will make it glow even brighter and more intensely. Only your own fear will try to extinguish it — if so just remember to draw more golden light into your heart and it can never be put out. Let fear go.
To close	:	**Imagine a spiral of white light come up from the earth below you, encircling you seven times, in a clockwise direction. When it gets to the top of your head, see it enter the top of your head and go back to the earth below you, via your spine. Be very aware of your feet on the ground or what you are lying upon.**
		I repeat — this is an important part of the exercise — it will "ground" you and help you feel less spaced out.

71

☼ Exercise Six

BREATHE IN THE SUN — TO THE ENERGY CENTRES
— TO THE BODY — CLOSE

Close your eyes

Let out a big sigh	:	As you do so think of yourself letting go of any stress or negative thought you are holding onto.
Repeat the sigh	:	Let it go.
Breathe in slowly	:	A deep breath in.
Breathe out slowly	:	As you do so, let go. Let go of all the troubles and trivia that you are holding in your mind at this time. Forget them. You do not need them at this time. This is your time. Let them go.
Repeat the slow breathing above		
Repeat again	:	Really let go of all these thoughts. Feel your body gently relaxing. Be at peace. If you need to, say it, "Be at peace."

Imagine you are sitting in the sunshine	:	Whether on your favourite beach, in a field, or garden, or woodland area — wherever you feel happiest.
Feel the warmth of the sun	:	Feel it on the top of your head, on your shoulders.
See that sun	:	See its golden light above you, with your imagination, with your mind.
See that golden light	:	See it just above the top of your head, again with your imagination.
Breathe in that sunlight to your forehead*	:	As you breathe in, imagine you are drawing down the golden light in through the top of your head. Keep your breathing relaxed. See it travel to your forehead. Leave it there for a few moments.
See that light travel down to your throat*	:	Imagine that light moving down to your throat area. Breathe in more light through the top of your head (the crown) if you feel you need to. Leave it there for a few moments.

See that light travel down to your heart*	: Again, breathe in more light if necessary, and leave it there, as above.
See that light travel down to your solar plexus*	: This is the area where the ribs part. Again, do as above.
See that light travel down to your lower abdomen* i.e. two inches below your navel	: This is known as the sacral area. Again, do as above.
See that light travel down to the base of your spine	: Again, do as above.
Bring down more of that golden light into your heart	: Breathe in more of that light through the top of your head and see it move, in your imagination, down to your heart.
Let the light expand in your heart	: Do this for a few moments.
Let that light expand and slowly spread to all parts of your body	: See your body filled with beautiful golden light.

Send more light
from your heart to
those areas of your
body you feel need
healing or a boost

To close   :   **Imagine a spiral of white
light come up from the earth
below you, encircling you
seven times, in a clockwise
direction. When it gets to the
top of your head, see it enter
the top of your head and go
back to the earth below you,
via your spine. Be very aware
of your feet on the ground or
what you are lying upon.**

I repeat — this is an important
part of the exercise — it will
"ground" you and help you
feel less spaced out.

*These areas, including the crown, are called the energy centres,
or chakras.*

☼ Exercise Seven

"THE LAKE OF PEACE"

Close your eyes

Let out a big sigh	:	As you do so think of yourself letting go of any stress or negative thought you are holding onto.
Repeat the sigh	:	Let it go.
Breathe in slowly	:	A deep breath in.
Breathe out slowly	:	As you do so, let go. Let go of all the troubles and trivia that you are holding in your mind at this time. Forget them. You do not need them at this time. This is your time. Let them go.
Repeat the slow breathing above		
Repeat again	:	Really let go of all these thoughts. Feel your body gently relaxing. Be at peace. If you need to, say it, "Be at peace."

Imagine you are sitting in the sunshine beside a beautiful still lake	:	In your mind picture yourself by this lovely lake. It is still and peaceful. Notice the deep blue of the water, reflecting the clear blue sky. You are warm and relaxed sitting by this lake.
Imagine the trees and the landscape surrounding this lake	:	In your mind, see the trees surrounding it, reflected in the water. Perhaps it is surrounded by beautiful hills. See the grass you are sitting on. See the wild flowers around you. Take in this scene and enjoy it.
Slowly breathe in the silence	:	The lake is perfectly still, and is peaceful and beautiful. Breathe in slowly and absorb into your body the silence.
Slowly breathe in the elements	:	Think of the peace of the water, the energy of fire and the earth, and the freedom of the wind. Feel the wind in your hair, the warmth of the sun, and the earth you are sitting upon. Feel the peace and silence of the lake. Think of yourself absorbing these elements as you breathe in.

Know that you can return to
this lake of peace whenever
you choose to do so and, as
you leave it, you take with
you its peace and tranquillity
into your physical life. It will
always be there for you when
you call upon it.

To close   :   **Imagine a spiral of white
light come up from the earth
below you, encircling you
seven times, in a clockwise
direction. When it gets to the
top of your head, see it enter
the top of your head and go
back to the earth below you,
via your spine. Be very aware
of your feet on the ground or
what you are lying upon.**

I repeat — this is an important
part of the exercise — it will
"ground" you and help you
feel less spaced out.

☼ Exercise Eight

"THE GARDEN"

Close your eyes

Let out a big sigh	:	As you do so think of yourself letting go of any stress or negative thought you are holding onto.
Repeat the sigh	:	Let it go.
Breathe in slowly	:	A deep breath in.
Breathe out slowly	:	As you do so, let go. Let go of all the troubles and trivia that you are holding in your mind at this time. Forget them. You do not need them at this time. This is your time. Let them go.
Repeat the slow breathing above		
Repeat again	:	Really let go of all these thoughts. Feel your body gently relaxing. Be at peace. If you need to, say it, "Be at peace."

Imagine before you a gate	:	Imagine you are standing before a gate. See its shape and size, and what it is made of.
Look through the gate	:	Beyond the gate is a beautiful garden. See its inviting beauty, the colours and form beyond.
Go through the gate	:	The gate opens and you step inside. Feel the grass beneath your feet. The garden is full of gorgeous flowers. The colours are vibrant and you wander amongst them, looking at the trees.
Sit down in a special place in the garden	:	You find a place in the garden where there is a seat, where you rest and feel the peace of the garden.
Your loved ones come to join you at this special place	:	As you are sitting there, you are joined by those you love, in this special meeting place. It does not matter whether they are still in this physical life or not. You embrace each other and you feel the love they have for you. They may or may not have something to tell you. Sit with them a while and enjoy this reunion.

Return to the gate	:	Embrace them one last time and leave this special place. Go back the way you came, past the trees and flowers until you find the gate.
Walk back through the gate	:	Take one last look at the garden and go through the gate, closing it behind you. Know that you can return to this garden and be with those you love whenever you need to.
To close	:	**Imagine a spiral of white light come up from the earth below you, encircling you seven times, in a clockwise direction. When it gets to the top of your head, see it enter the top of your head and go back to the earth below you, via your spine. Be very aware of your feet on the ground or what you are lying upon.**

I repeat — this is an important part of the exercise — it will "ground" you and help you feel less spaced out.

☼ Exercise Nine

"THE SPECIAL FRIEND"

Close your eyes

Let out a big sigh	:	As you do so think of yourself letting go of any stress or negative thought you are holding onto.
Repeat the sigh	:	Let it go.
Breathe in slowly	:	A deep breath in.
Breathe out slowly	:	As you do so, let go. Let go of all the troubles and trivia that you are holding in your mind at this time. Forget them. You do not need them at this time. This is your time. Let them go.
Repeat the slow breathing above		
Repeat again	:	Really let go of all these thoughts. Feel your body gently relaxing. Be at peace. If you need to, say it, "Be at peace."

Imagine before you a gate	:	Imagine you are standing before a gate. See its shape and size, and what it is made of.
Look through the gate	:	Beyond the gate is a beautiful garden. See its inviting beauty, the colours and form beyond.
Go through the gate	:	The gate opens and you step inside. Feel the grass beneath your feet. The garden is full of gorgeous flowers. The colours are vibrant and you wander amongst them, looking at the trees.
Sit down in a special place in the garden	:	You find a place in the garden where there is a seat, where you rest and feel the peace of the garden.
You are joined by a special friend	:	As you are sitting there, you are joined by someone you may not have met before, but know is your special friend. That person has such great love for you and you feel that love shining out from his/her heart for you. You may or may not see their face, it does not matter. Feel their presence, and enjoy the love and peace they bring you.

Your friend has a special gift for you	:	Your friend gives you a present. It is wrapped up. See its wrapping. Notice its colour and texture. Feel the love with which it comes.
Open your gift	:	You slowly remove its wrapping, and open it. You look at what is inside. It may have a significance for you. Look at it carefully. Feel it in your hands.
Ask your friend if they have a message for you	:	Do not be afraid to ask your friend if they have a message for you. They may not, the gift may be all you need right now.
Thank your friend and return to the gate	:	Bid farewell to your friend and thank him/her for what they have given you. Know that this friend is always there for you and you take the love back with you into the physical world. Go back through the garden until you find the gate.

Walk back through the gate	:	Take one last look at the garden and go through the gate, closing it behind you. Know that you can return to this garden and meet your friend whenever you need to.
To close	:	**Imagine a spiral of white light come up from the earth below you, encircling you seven times, in a clockwise direction. When it gets to the top of your head, see it enter the top of your head and go back to the earth below you, via your spine. Be very aware of your feet on the ground or what you are lying upon.**

I repeat — this is an important part of the exercise — it will "ground" you and help you feel less spaced out.

☼ Exercise Ten

"THE HEALING FOUNTAIN"

Close your eyes

Let out a big sigh	:	As you do so think of yourself letting go of any stress or negative thought you are holding onto.
Repeat the sigh	:	Let it go.
Breathe in slowly	:	A deep breath in.
Breathe out slowly	:	As you do so, let go. Let go of all the troubles and trivia that you are holding in your mind at this time. Forget them. You do not need them at this time. This is your time. Let them go.
Repeat		
Repeat again	:	Really let go of all these thoughts. Feel your body gently relaxing. Be at peace. If you need to, say it, "Be at peace."

Imagine before you a gate	:	Imagine you are standing before a gate. See its shape and size, and what it is made of.
Look through the gate	:	Beyond the gate is a beautiful garden. See its inviting beauty, the colours and form beyond.
Go through the gate	:	The gate opens and you step inside. Feel the grass beneath your feet. The garden is full of gorgeous flowers. The colours are vibrant and you wander amongst them, looking at the trees.
You find a beautiful fountain	:	You come across a beautiful fountain, with water that sparkles in the sunlight. You sit by it and feel at peace as you gaze upon it.
You take a cup and drink from the fountain	:	By the fountain, there is a golden cup. You fill the cup with water from the fountain. See the water sparkling with light in your cup. Drink it. It is full of healing energy and love. It is your medicine. Know that it contains all you

need. Feel its goodness and healing power as you drink it. Accept the healing it gives you. Be at peace.

Return to the gate : Go back through the garden, past the flowers and trees until you find the gate.

Walk back through : Take one last look at the the gate garden and go through the gate, closing it behind you. Know that you can return to this healing fountain whenever you want to.

To close : **Imagine a spiral of white light come up from the earth below you, encircling you seven times, in a clockwise direction. When it gets to the top of your head, see it enter the top of your head and go back to the earth below you, via your spine. Be very aware of your feet on the ground or what you are lying upon.**

I repeat — this is an important part of the exercise — it will "ground" you and help you feel less spaced out.

Postscript

(A Little Bird Told Me...)

In January or February 1997, I was in my bathroom at midnight. I had been there for a few minutes, when suddenly there was a tap, tap, tapping at the window-pane right by my side. The roller blind was down and as we lived in a remote farmhouse it was pitch black outside.

The tapping continued without a break for a minute or so. I thought the wind must have got up and the branches of the hawthorn tree outside were scraping against the window-pane. Then, however, I remembered that the gardener had recently cut it back, so it could not be that.

I gingerly lifted the corner of the roller blind and was astonished to see a little bird, a thrush with its beautiful spotted chest, sitting on the window ledge tapping its beak at the bottom corner of the window-pane right by me. I thought birds were usually asleep at this time, but even more amazing was that it was unphased by my action and it was only inches from me on the other side of the glass. These birds are wild, not tame, and are usually shy of humans.

As it saw me, it cocked its head to one side and then to the other, again and again as if it was trying to tell me something, whilst looking me straight in the eyes. I talked to it through the glass and I felt a rush of excitement and good feeling. It was there for three or four minutes, with me talking to it and it cocking its head at me to each side as if responding in a conversation, before it flew away. I knew it was bringing me good news of some kind.

I have always had an affinity with birds and they have brought me news before, though usually of the births and deaths in the family kind of news. I had been wanting to move house for a long time to a particular kind of house and this time I thought it was about that. As it turned out, within a matter of weeks, the right house came on the market and we did in fact move within a few months. That move was the first of many major changes in my life over the next two years.

A couple of years later, and a few days after I had finished this book, I was cooking tea for my children in the kitchen of the house where I now live when, for some reason, I became aware that two birds were sitting on the TV aerial on the chimney of the house opposite. About five minutes later, one of them flew down and started pecking at the bottom corner of the window-pane, whilst fluttering its wings as if to get my attention.

It was another thrush. It kept doing this fluttering and pecking and the children were amazed. It settled on the window ledge looking at me in the eyes, cocking its head at me like the one before and I got a rush of excitement. I felt it was about this book. The bird was there for about a minute fluttering and pecking and then it flew back up to its perch on the TV aerial next to its mate. They flew off together and I did not see it again.

A few days later, after this incident, I went to see my friend Anna Wilson nearby. She is a wonderful healer who has an amazing gift of clairvoyance. I told her of my book, its title and then I told her what had happened regarding the bird and asked her what she thought.

She said that the hairs on her neck were standing on end as just minutes before I had arrived a bird flew at the window-pane of the room in which she was healing, with such force that there was a terrific bang. She looked out of the window and saw it on the ground. She thought it was a thrush. She thought the bird must have been killed and she went outside to see if it was dead, but there was no sign of it when she got there. Furthermore, each of her two patients she had seen before my arrival that morning had used the words "the wider picture". She too had never before heard that phrase. She felt that it was good news about the book and that it would be published.

A co-incidence?